Accessorizing Computers
What Comes Out of the Box is a Really Just a Starter Kit

Yesterday, we spent about three hours trying to convince a client of ours that brand new computers just don't come equipped with the all things that most computers need in a PC. We tried to convince him that a fully functional computer is one that is personalized with specially selected hardware and software accessories - and that the computer purchased at the store doesn't come with these things. Unfortunately, all of our convincing was to our avail. Our client insisted that he should never need more than what came with his boxed product and that we were just trying "bilk" more money out of him.

As computer consultants, it's our job and mission to make sure our clients are 100% satisfied when they walk out our offices. But our job is unnecessarily made harder when people don't take the time to learn about computer accessories and familiarize themselves with the limitations of store-bought computers. Hopefully by the time you finish reading this article, you'll understand the lesson that we were trying to teach our client: "What comes out of the box is really just a starter kit."

The typical computer package comes with a CPU unit, keyboard, mouse, and speaker set. That may be just fine for some, but most people require more than that especially in today's "connected" society. Today's users require full multimedia capabilities, a wide range of graphics tools, and accommodations for the various portables we now enjoy. These extras aren't included with "what comes out of the box," and the only way to get them is to accessorize.

To illustrate the importance of accessorizing, we like to use the "plain dough" analogy. Let's say that a brand new computer is a batch of plain dough – waiting to be flavored and baked into something useful. If we want to use this dough to make a delicious batch of chocolate chip cookies, we would need to "accessorize" this dough with chocolate chips and a little brown sugar. If we want to use this dough into in a warm loaf of sesame seed bread on the other hand, we'd need to "accessorize" the dough with yeast and sesame seeds.

Like "plain dough," the brand new computer isn't very useful by itself. It needs accessorizing.

Depending on what's needed, accessorizing doesn't need to be expensive. In fact, you can get away with paying a minimal amount for extra software and hardware if these accessories are for children. It's when these accessories are work requirements or when they're needed to produce works of quality for any other reason that they can become rather expensive. And this expense applies to microphones, digital cameras, PDAs, scanners, video cams, and more.

Regardless of cost, it's important to understand that accessories can become "necessities," and that the best time to get them is the moment you buy a new computer. Waiting too long to accessorize can cause more problems than necessary because while you wait, manufacturers continuously develop new technologies – technologies that your computer won't be able to accommodate in the future. Once you're ready to accessorize, the new products on the market are too advanced for your computer and they just won't work. This is a typical problem experienced by those who want to use hardware designed for

Windows Vista on a Windows XP or Windows 2000 machine.

Automating Things with Batch Files

They Work on Today's Computers Too!

If you're familiar with MS-DOS at all, you'll recall that it's a command-driven operating system that performs functions issued at the C:> prompt. The only way to get an MS-DOS computer to do something was to type a command at this prompt and if you can imagine, it was a rather cumbersome way to use a computer.

As an example, to load up Microsoft's simple editing program, you had to type the name of the drive that the program was on, the directory that the program was in, and then the name of the program. So if Microsoft Edit was in a directory or folder named "Process," you could start the program by typing, "C:>process\edit.com" Then, and only then would the program load up for use.

This is a small command, but just imagine if you had a program that was deeply nested within a series of folder. You could end up typing a command as wide as your computer screen or worse, long enough that the entire command would have to wrap onto the next line! Now imagine having to type these long commands every time that you wanted to start a program. Yikes!

That's one of the reasons why batch files became so popular. Batch files are small text-based documents that contain a bunch of these commands on their own lines. When executed, they would process each command without the user having to type each and every one of them.

When Windows was developed, the need for typing commands was essentially eradicated thanks to the introduction of the point-and-click (mouse) interface. But this didn't stop the batch file fever that started under MS-DOS – and in some small circles, batch files are still as popular as they were in the beginning.

Even though you may use Windows XP or Vista, batch files can save you tons of time by automatically starting multiple programs and performing different tasks at the single click of a button. They don't require any extensive programming background and they don't need to be encrypted with some weird, expensive compiler. Batch files are plain text files, and you can build one for your own personal use with Windows' Notepad.

You could make a batch file that loads up your favorite websites at once for example, or you could make a batch file that fills your desktop with the most important applications for the day. To do so only requires a little knowledge about the locations of these applications.

Let's say that every day we need to load up the Yahoo web browser, Microsoft Word, and then the calculator that comes with Windows. Instead of doing this by hand, we could write a batch file to do it for us.

First, we'd load up Notepad and type in the following:

START "http://www.yahoo.com"

START "c:/program files/microsoft office/office/winword.exe"

START "c:/windows/calc.exe"

We would then save this data into a file named, "mytasks.bat" onto the Desktop for easy access. Each time we double-clicked on this file, the Yahoo website would load up, Microsoft Word would start, and the simple calculator would pop up.

Since we want these programs to load every day, we could create a shortcut to this file and then place the shortcut inside our computer's Start Up folder. That way, these three programs would load every time we turn on the computer. If you wanted these programs to start minimized, you could type the following into a batch file instead:

START http://www.yahoo.com /m

START "c:/program files/microsoft office/office/winword.exe" /m

START "c:/windows/calc.exe" /m

This will run all three programs as before, however the "/m" parameter will minimize them so that they don't clutter up the desktop.

Other people have found much more creative and effective ways to use batch files, but the important thing is that you know they're a resource you can use to save a few seconds or minutes in performing important tasks. We've come a long way from MS-DOS, but it's still a valuable source of automation that anyone can use with no programming knowledge at all.

Basic GUI Terminology
Knowing What You're Working With Helps Technicians

Getting help with your computer software can be easier when you know the correct terms to use. One of the biggest problems that new computer users have with technical support is not knowing how to correctly describe the problem that they're having. And it isn't fair to expect a tech support person to automatically know what a "thing-a-ma-jingy," or "whatcha-ma-call-it" is.

The following describes the correct names for common components of software so that when you experience a problem, you can effectively describe an issue that you're having and a technician can readily resolve it.

User interface – this is the visual design of a program. It may contain squares, boxes, words, icons, and buttons. If you're experiencing insufficient memory for example, you might see black rectangles across the *user interface* of your software programs.

Title bar – this is the top-most part of a program that displays its own name or it may describe the contents displayed in another part of the interface. If a program is incorrectly coded, you may see a wrong description in this part of its interface.

Menu bar - this part of a program displays menu items and menu options. Some of the most common parts of a menu bar grants access to File commands, Open commands, Save commands, and Print commands. An example of an error in this part of an interface would be if an option was missing or grayed out (lighter in color).

Tool bar – this part of a program displays small icons across the top which represent tools. Clicking an icon will open a tool or process a command that might also exist on a program's menu bar. Problems in this part of an interface are uncommon, however if you find yourself repeatedly clicking an icon with no results, you can correctly describe the problem by referring to the *toolbar*.

Minimize, Restore, and Exit buttons – these three buttons are usually located on the right-most upper part of a program's interface and each allow you to minimize a program's screen, restore it to its original size, or shut down the program completely.

Scroll bar – this convenient tool allows users to move data up and down the computer screen.

Status bar – this part of a program is located at the bottom-most part of its interface, and it usually displays small messages that indicate the progress of a command or task. If programmed incorrectly, an application might display the wrong information in this area.

Context menu – like the menu bar, a context menu displays when a user right-clicks on something. It displays commands just like what you see on a File menu or a Help menu.

Input box – input boxes are usually small rectangles that allow you to type data into a simple interfaces like a webpage or browser window. If you find that you can't type information into one of these, you can effectively resolve the issue with a technician by calling it an input box, rather than a "white rectangle," or "place to put in text."

Button – buttons perform a command after a user clicks them with a mouse. Problems occur when the text of a button is grayed out or if it doesn't appear to sink into the screen when clicked.

Check box – a check box is a small box that allows a user to indicate several choices among many. When clicked, a small "x" displays inside a box. Similar to the check box, a **radio button** allows a user to indicate a single choice among many. Problems with radio buttons and check boxes occur when a user makes one choice, but the interface reacts as if the user made many choices (or none at all). When describing a problem to a technician, be sure to indicate whether the problem occurs with a check box or a radio box. Computer novices mistakenly interchange the names of both of these controls.

Buying a Computer

What To Do And Why

It isn't fair, but buying a computer is just plain easier for some than it is for others. Those who've purchased and used a computer in the past already have an idea of what they need in a new computer. But those who are new to the computer world could get lost in the myriad of choices available.

The short answer to "What should I buy?" is "The best." Of course that answer is extremely subjective because "the best" to one person is certainly different to another. Our definition of "the best" is the fastest and the biggest, but even that leaves the computer newbie confused. Here's a quick rundown of what the computer novice should do and why.

1. Buy a computer that includes basic peripherals. Every computer can be broken down into four major components: CPU unit, monitor, keyboard, and mouse. For the novice, it's best to buy a computer that has all of these components included so that when it's taken home, assembling the computer is a simple matter of plugging things in where they belong. Save the individual

purchases of these components for those who have more experience.

2. Decide what you'll use the computer for. If you want to use your computer for cruising the web, sending email, or performing simple word-processing or spreadsheet tasks, a computer with the basic components that we just described should suffice. If you want to use a computer to help with a career in multimedia however, you're going to need to accessorize your system with a scanner, printer, digital camera, tablet, or digicam for example. If you want a computer to help with a career in music, you will need a quality microphone and set of speakers.

3. Create a budget and stick to it. How much can you afford to spend on a new computer? Although the prices of computers are decreasing, they can still create a hefty expense especially if you need additional peripherals described above. In addition, you'll need to figure in costs for maintenance, servicing, and insuring.

4. Start comparison shopping and look for the "fastest and biggest." By "fastest and biggest," we mean the computer with the fastest processor, the fastest modem, the biggest memory, and the biggest hard drive capacity. Even if you think that you'll never need the amount of speed or space available on the market today, it's important to

have in the event that you truly do need that much in the future. Having such a large reserve will cut down on costs when the time comes to upgrade for more than what you may settle for in a computer that offers less.

5. Stick with the better-known brands. Venturing off the beaten path with lessor-known brands is again, an adventure for those who have more experience with computers. Although those better-known brands may be a tad bit more expensive, the computer novice will appreciate the comfort in purchasing a computer from a business that has a long record of building quality products, and that has the funds available for fulfilling returns, trades, servicing, and warranties.

6. Select a store. Having an idea of what you want in a computer and what kind of computer that you want, your only task left is to select the place in which you want to buy it. There are a number of places available including computer store outlets, online stores, auction sites, used computer stores, or your friendly neighborhood yard sale. For the computer novice, we recommend buying a computer from a physical store. In a physical store, you have the opportunity to see the computer of interest in person and ask questions. New computer buyers also have access to store warranties, returns, trades, and services.

These suggestions should give the computer newbie a great start in selecting a quality computer for the first time and they apply to either Windows computers or Apple Macintosh computers. After making these decisions and finally selecting one that fits your needs, you can then venture into the fascinating world of software – a world that is just as grand as the world of hardware!

Cheap and Fast Software
An Introduction to Shareware

Visit any computer store today and you'll find what seems like miles and miles of software on sale. Certainly enticing buys, there are a few problems with buying software off the shelves. On the shelf, software – otherwise known as "commercial software" - can be expensive, and incompatible, and outdated when compared to what's available online. Fortunately, there's an alternative to commercial software and although it isn't new, it's one of the most under-exploited opportunities in the computer industry.

We're talking about shareware – software that you can try before buying.

Shareware has a long history and was rather popular in the days where BBS (bulletin board systems) reigned the online industry. It hasn't gone anywhere, but its competition with commercial software is fierce – so fierce that it tends to fall on the back burner among new computer users. This is unfortunate because shareware has so many advantages over commercial software.

One of those advantages is its cost. On the whole, shareware is generally cheaper than commercial software. But don't misinterpret the cost. With shareware, cheap does not equal low-quality and there are plenty of examples that prove shareware often outperforms the quality of commercial software time and time again. How much savings are we talking about? You could purchase a quality word processor, spreadsheet, database program, or system utility anywhere from a mere $15 to under a hundred. This is almost unheard of in stores like Best Buy, Circuit City, or Egghead, yet the shareware programs offered within this price range rival even Microsoft's Office suite.

Another advantage that shareware has over commercial software is its compatibility. We're not saying that shareware is compatible with all operating systems. What we're saying is that since we can try shareware before paying for it, we can determine if the software is completely compatible with our systems first. In other words, we can discover whether the software performs the way we want them to and should anyone try to do the same with commercial software, they'll be in for a big disappointment.

Commercial software policy doesn't even allow for returns, let alone "borrowing" them to try them.

The last advantage that shareware has over commercial software (but certainly not the least) is its applicability. Plain and simple, shareware is the best bet when you want to keep on top of the latest release of a particular program. Sure, computer stores do their best to keep their inventory up to date, but when you can download version 5.6042 of a shareware program as opposed to buying a commercial 3.0 version from the local computer shop, there's just no comparison.

Which brings up our next point. Just where does one get shareware? Shareware is all over the Internet and it's really hard not to bump into it. The most popular places to find shareware is within thousands of download libraries, however the companies (and even independent programmers behind shareware) are increasingly offering shareware from their own websites. A simple Google or Yahoo search for a particular type of program will yield all sorts of results that point you toward items that you can try before you buy.

Be aware however, that because shareware is not commercial software, you may not experience a full program the way you would if you bought the software out of a box. Shareware may or may not be limited – meaning that some functions may not be available to you until the program is paid for. These limitations are often small and don't interfere with the way its full version operations. They're really just implemented as a way to prompt payment. Remember that shareware is not freeware. You shouldn't try to use shareware as commercial software without paying for it.

About the only thing that's similar between shareware and commercial software is the way in which they may be bought. With a credit card, you can be the new owner of your own software within minutes.

A Few Common Computer Errors

(And What They Mean)

Computer errors can pop up when least expected, they can cau the entire system to suddenly shut down, and they can inadvertently corrupt data to the point where it can't be deciphered. Although they can't always be avoided, it's import to remember that computer errors can be corrected. The key is t understand what computer errors are, understand what they m when they show up, and understand how to minimize their occurrence in the first place.

Basically, computer errors are the result of a number of things t may or may not have anything to do with the way the compute used. They "operate" whenever there's a conflict among commands. Remember that computers essentially run off of a se of commands and it's usually a smooth process. But when one command conflicts with another command – or when one command asks for a process or information that isn't available, t computer returns results that aren't useable. That's an error.

A prime example of this kind of error is when users attempt to u software that isn't applicable for their system. Almost all softwar accompanies a list of system requirements which dictates what a computer needs to have in order for the software to work properly. To minimize errors of this sort, always verify that your computer has the required components. A project management program that you're interested in may require a specific operating system, like Windows XP for example. And although this program may install just fine on a Windows 98 machine, it will generate a multitude of errors once its started.

Insufficient memory will cause errors as well. That's why software programs include minimum memory requirements. A program that needs 14MB of memory will generate errors on a computer that only has 4MB of memory if it runs at all. The same goes for disk space, monitor color depth and resolution. In these situations, problems occur the moment that a piece of software attempts to access the things (hardware, memory, space, resolution, etc.) that it cannot find.

Because some programs share common files, errors can also occur when these shared files are not up to date. For instance, let's say that Program A is already installed on a computer and it's working just fine. Then let's say that the user of that computer downloads and installs Program B. Program B uses a file that Program A installed much earlier, but when Program B is run, errors popup. Those errors are the result of Program B attempting to use an outdated (shared) file that was installed by Program A. In order to fix that problem, the user would have to download an updated version of the shared file (which to say the least – is not an easy thing to find or do).

Sometimes, errors occur because a system doesn't have the required drivers or the drivers that are on the system are the incorrect version. Both errors in these cases can be resolved by updating the computer on a regular basis. Microsoft provides a section on its website that can automatically update a computer online and it does this at no cost in an effort to reduce errors like this. Always try to keep your computer updated so that should a program share a file, it will share a file that has been updated on hundreds of thousands of computers, like yours.

This article doesn't even begin to cover the entire gamut of computer errors – but additional information regarding how to help with a computer issue (including computer errors) can be found in our article titled, "Computer Help" no matter what the problem is.

Computer Help
Where and How to Get It

Well there's no denying it – No matter how new or how well maintained our computers are, we all encounter computer problems sooner or later. The good news is that we don't have to face them alone. There are a ton of resources available to walk us through computer issues but it may take a little knowledge in knowing how to access them. This article will show you how.

1. Remember help files. It's funny, but people seem to forget that every computer and every program installed on a computer comes with its own help file. Even the operating system of a computer has a help file and it really should be the first place to look for answers. Help files are designed not only to guide the usage of a computer, they're also designed to solve problems. Inside a help file, look for a section called, "Troubleshooting" (or something similar) when you need to resolve an issue. This section is reserved for solving problems specific to the software or hardware that you're using.

2. Product websites. If you're having a problem with a piece of software or with a hardware part, try

the website of that software's or hardware's manufacturer. Most (if not all) manufacturer's reserve a portion of cyberspace and dedicate it to support the products that they build. Microsoft's help desk is good example.

3. Fan sites. Fan sites probably isn't a good name for this resource, but you can find websites that are dedicated toward supporting the users of a particular software program or piece of hardware. We've called them "fan sites" because the maintainers of these sites have no affiliation with the manufacturers that they support! Call them what you will, but their free help is immeasurable and without it, we wouldn't have some of the wonderful workarounds and unique problem solving techniques that we have today.

4. Usenet newsgroups. Another underused resource on the Internet, Usenet newsgroups have hundreds of discussion groups dedicated to some of the most popular computer systems, operating systems, hardware manufacturers, and individual software programs. Sometimes, the representatives of these companies participate, but most of the time, the support in this group is user to user, which is just as valid because you're working with a team of experienced people.

5. Support Lines. Another source for help that we shouldn't forget are the support systems of

various manufacturers. You can reach these systems by calling the phone number associated with the product that you're having trouble with. Calls may be free (1-800 or 1-877 number), or they may cost a small fee (1-900).

6. PC support groups or user groups are another option for help. These are groups that meet in libraries, computer stores, or other local areas and they discuss all sorts of issues related with a particular product. Even if you aren't experiencing a computer or software problem, user groups are fun to participate in and they can help you network into other interests such as job or teaching opportunities.

7. Surprisingly, you may even get a helping hand from the salespersons at your local computer store. We don't recommend that you make this your first pit stop when you experience a problem, but we don't recommend that you rule this option out altogether either. Computer salespersons are hired for a reason – and that's their knowledge. Often, these kind folks can help you resolve an issue over the phone and prevent you form having to buy a costly solution.

As you can see, help is easy to find - You've just got to know where to look for it. Most of the contacts within these resources are extremely friendly and willing to take the time to walk you through a problem at little to no cost. From online discussion groups to the files on your own computer, help is often just a click away.

Computer Security
In Today's Society, Protecting Your Computer Is A
Requirement

Advances in computer technology is a double-edged sword. On one hand, it affords us quick and easy access to numerous conveniences such as bank statements, favorite shopping centers, school and health records, and more. On the other hand, it can also grant the same access to those who aren't supposed to get it. Although it's a rare occurrence, hacking has become the biggest criminal nuisance in computer history.

Make no bones about it. There's nothing innocent or cute about the hacker. Today's hackers aren't the pimply-faced teen rebels that you might be thinking of. Instead, this generation of hackers are grown individuals who are more than likely earning a living by stealing the identities of innocent, law abiding individuals and then selling those identities to others who want to slip by the system. And the only protection against these seedy people is prevention.

Computer security couldn't be more important than it is today and that's why we've taken the time to introduce it to you. You can reduce the probability of experiencing identity theft by making your computer as hacker-proof as possible. All that's needed is a little software and a lot of common sense.

1. Install an anti-virus/anti-spyware program. Anti-virus/anti-spyware software will stop malicious code from downloading and installing onto your computer while you peruse the Internet. Known as viruses, worms, or spyware, this malicious code can destroy important files and render your computer good for only one thing: sending sensitive data back to the server of an identity thief.

2. Don't store sensitive data on your computer in the first place. Should your computer get infected with a virus, worm, or piece of spyware, you can thwart the individuals responsible by not storing your personal information on your PC so that when and if your computer does send back data – it won't be anything valuable. Hackers look for things like full names, social security numbers, phone numbers, home addresses, work-related information, and credit card numbers. If these things aren't saved onto a computer, there's nothing critical to worry about other than

restoring your computer to a non-virus condition.

3. Don't open files without scanning them with an anti-virus/anti-spyware program. In the past, the warning was to avoid opening files from people that you don't know. Today it's really not safe to open files from anyone (without scanning the files) because that's how viruses get spread – through files - even by mistake. So even though your co-worker may have emailed a funny video, it's no more safe to open than a video downloaded from a complete stranger. Be safe and scan each and every file you download from the Internet or receive through email regardless of where it came from.

4. Create a barrier between your computer and prying eyes. Anti-virus/anti-spyware programs are only effective after the effect. But you can prevent identity theft from occurring by installing a firewall. A firewall is software that checks all data entering and exiting a computer and it then blocks that which doesn't meet specified security criteria (user-defined rules).[1]

5. Don't click on website links in spam messages. In an effort to obtain personal information, some spammers will send email that asks you to click on a link. The email messages are often disguised as

---

important messages from well-known online establishments, and they often try to scare their readers into clicking links with threats of closing an account of some sort. Sometimes the links are harmless and attempt to con the reader into volunteering personal information (credit card number), but other times the links attempt to download harmful software onto a computer.

Your best protection against computer crimes is your own knowledge. Hopefully the suggestions above will prompt you into taking appropriate action and into protecting your computer with the suggested tools. In doing so, you'll not only protect yourself, you'll prevent the spread of these malicious activities and protect others at the same time.

Customizing Your Computer with Preferences
Making Your Computer Work with You - Not
Against You

Although you did not design or build your computer, you can turn it into a device that responds to your way of using it as if you were its original engineer or programmer. This is because the computer is a mere platform - a blank canvas, if you will - waiting for you to direct its operation or paint the picture of the perfect machine. All this is possible from making just a few changes in your computer's current configuration.

Your computer's main configurations are housed in Windows Control Panel. Within this small section of Windows, you can make some major changes from the way that your computer looks to the way that your computer responds to the people who use it. But your specifications don't just apply to Windows, they also apply to the many software programs that are installed onto the computer (not to mention that many software programs can be further customized through their own configurations). We aren't going to cover them all, but we will introduce some of the most popular so that you can get a feel of the control over your system that these configurations give you.

Users. Before we get into the individual settings, it's important that you understand that each set of configurations you make is specific to the users that sit down in front of a computer. Changes made to a system by one person will differ from the changes made by another. Enabled by a username and password, individual desktop settings (icons, background picture, and other settings) are available after logging onto Windows.

Display Properties. Through Display Properties, a user can change the background of the Windows Desktop, add a screensaver, change the overall color scheme and fonts of Windows, and adjust a computer's color depth and/or resolution (screen area). Not just a bunch of preference settings, display properties help individuals who have to deal with visual problems.

Accessibility Options. Speaking of visual problems, another setting that's useful is accessibility options. This setting allows people with disabilities to use a computer that accommodates vision and hearing problems.

Keyboard and Mouse Options. The keyboard and mouse controls give users the option of speeding up or slowing down the movements of both of these peripherals. For those entering the United States from a foreign country, users will appreciate how Windows grants use of keyboard layouts native to their original language. Other uses will appreciate the different selection of cursors and the ability to add additional ones.

Passwords. Since the computer in use may be shared with others, Passwords gives the almighty administrator the means to determine whether all users will share the same preferences and desktop settings or if users can customize preferences and desktop settings.

Regional Settings. Things get really personal in Regional Settings - as this configuration makes changes according to a user's location and language. Options available can accommodate a person's preference for the display of numbers, currency, time, and date format.

Sounds Properties. Multimedia fans can create a rich PC environment filled with sound through this setting. Sounds can be assigned to numerous events and they don't even need to be the default sounds installed by Windows. Users can download sounds from the Internet or create their own sounds with a microphone.

Dialing Properties. Even the way a user connects to the Internet can be customized. Through Dialing Properties, users can determine how a phone and modem dials into an Internet service provider.

From just these basic configuration options, you can create your own experience with a computer each time you sit down in front of one. Customizing your PC is what makes using a computer truly unique and enjoyable, so have fun and build a situation at home or a work in which you'll love to work with everyday. Should you feel a little nervous about it at first, remember that your computer's original configuration can be saved to a back up file should you ever want to restore it to the same state that it was in when you first bought it.

Dust Kills
Cleaning the Unit Fan is Essential Computer Care

Between taking care of the household, the kids, the pets, and the district PTA, computer care is probably one of the last things that you think of doing on a regular basis. Without a regular maintenance schedule however, you could find out (the hard way) that a neglected computer is an energy hog – one that works harder than it needs to and one that could be a financial burden to replace.

Let's talk about maintaining hardware. So much emphasis is put on maintaining a computer's operating system that we sometimes forget how important it is to maintain a computer's hardware components. Since there can be quite a few components to take care of, let's talk about the most important one.

The most important component of a computer's hardware system is its fan. The fan is located on the computer's CPU unit and when that thing gets clogged with dirt and dust, it can run down a computer faster than you can say, "Something's wrong with my computer and I don't know what it is!" In short, the fan is responsible for keeping a computer's motor cool and this motor is what keeps the computer's hard drive and peripherals functioning the way you need them to, which translates to "fast."

A dirty fan doesn't rotate fast enough to keep that motor cool and a completely clogged fan just stops rotating altogether. This causes the computer's motor to work harder - and a harder working motor can raise the electric bill! Worst case scenario: the motor can overheat and stop working as well. No motor equals no computer.

Keep your computer's fan clean by preventing the fan from getting dirty or dusty in the first place. Use the computer in a dust-free environment and never smoke around it. Nicotine and tar mean certain death when it comes to computer fans, however should you find a need to clean the fan, do so with extreme care.

It's quite easy to cause more damage from cleaning so if you're not comfortable with cleaning your PC yourself, take it to a shop for servicing. Otherwise, you can unplug and disassemble the computer to do it yourself.

You'll need a can of compressed air and an anti-static rag to remove stubborn clumps of dust. Hold the can perfectly vertical and spray the fan being careful not to spray the dust off the fan onto other sensitive parts of the computer like circuit boards or inside the motor casing. Wipe up remaining dust with your anti-static rag and then reassemble the computer.

One thing that you certainly don't want to use to remove computer dust is a vacuum cleaner. Although using a vacuum cleaner seems to make more sense, the strong suction of a vacuum cleaner can actually spark damaging static electricity or dislodge loose cables. You also don't want to use oil-based cleaners. Although Pledge may dust your wooden tables and cabinets to a perfect shine, the oil inside a cleaner like this will erode sensitive computer parts. Stick to a liquid-free dusting method and your dusting routine will be safe enough to repeat as often as you need.

As previously mentioned, preventing dust from entering the computer is extremely important and will reduce the need to open and dust your system in the first place. The severity of outside elements (smoking, humidity, pets, etc.) will ultimately determine how often you'll need to de-dust your machine. But as an average, you shouldn't need to perform this procedure any more than once or twice a year.

The entire exercise should take no more than twenty minutes tops and once complete, you'll immediately see and hear the difference in your machine. The computer's keyboard and mouse will run more smoothly, hardware won't take as long to connect, and the entire machine won't be as loud as one that's corroded with ugly dust bunnies.

Programs Included With a New Computer
Are they good enough to stand on their own?

The Windows operating systems already comes with a useful collection of pre-installed programs and even some games. But one of the first things that people do is download a butt-load of new programs as soon as a brand new system is plugged in the wall and connected to the Internet. This article looks at some of the programs that are included with most new systems and then asks the reader to consider if they're sufficient.

NotePad and WordPad. All Windows systems include the two text editors, "NotePad," and "WordPad." Notepad is a plain text editor while WordPad is a rich text editor. Both files are capable of opening plain text, however WordPad can open Windows Write files (an earlier version of WordPad) as well as rich text files. WordPad can also save documents as plain text, rich text, and MS Word documents. So with WordPad having the ability to read and create rich text; embed objects (sound, pictures, and video); and manipulate fonts, we have to wonder if other word processors, which do the same thing, are really necessary. Although WordPad is certainly no match for Microsoft Word's internal spell and grammar checker or Word's Internet linking capabilities, we believe it's a great introduction to word processing in general for computer novices.

Address Book. There are hoards of advanced contact database programs floating around the Internet and on store shelves, but Windows provides a completely competent contact database of its own simply known as "Address Book." This small compact utility allows users to organize contacts by name, location, group, or number and it give users ample space to fully describe each. Compared to Microsoft's Access database program, its user-friendly Address Book is a Godsend to new computer users.

Calculator. Calculator has been a Windows accessory even from its first debut in Windows 1.0. For the life of us, we can't figure out why anyone other than a rocket scientist would want to install a different version than this free one that comes pre-installed. Windows calculator has two interfaces: an easy one, and a scientific one. So perhaps a rocket scientist could fare well with Windows Calculator after all!

Paint. Windows' Paint program allows users to make changes to existing graphics, or create brand new ones at no additional cost. Interestingly, we can count at least ten different graphics packages that are more popular and widely used than this free one. While it doesn't offer as many editing tools, it does provide the essentials and it can open/save graphics in .bmp, .gif, and.jpg format (the latter two being the most commonly format used for Internet eye candy).

Media Player. Real Player and QuickTime are the first programs we think of when we think about multimedia. But Windows Media Player, also free and pre-installed, does a fine job at transmitting Internet-bound sound and video. With this application, you can easily listen to .wav files, .midi files, and even tune into a little Internet radio if you like.

System Tools. Although there are too many to list here, Windows provides more than a handful of useful utilities that will monitor system resources, organize files, repair damaged disks, and more. Yet and still, you can easily find similar tools for sale at computer outlets and download libraries.

What's going on here?

The truth of the matter is that the programs pre-installed are great tools for the beginning computer user. At some point down the road, usage will dictate a need for more powerful applications. We may need a word processor that can convert a document into an HTML page or PDF document. We may need a calculator that solves geometric problems. Or we may need a multimedia tool that lets us create our own videos as well as watch them. These capabilities aren't included with new systems, but there's no reason why we can't exploit the tools that we're given to their fullest.

Introduction to Programming
Controlling Your Computer with a Programming
Language

In a previous article, we introduced automating some
tasks with MS-DOS batch files. In this article, we're
going to introduce programming and describe how it
can be used to control the way your computer works.
Normally, computer novices aren't interested in
controlling the computer. New computer users are
typically interested in learning more about how the
thing works. However they may be surprised to learn
that programming increases computer knowledge as
a whole and it can help to diminish the fear associated
with using a new computer.

Programming a computer is creating a sequence of
instructions that enable the computer to do
something.[2] The people who program computers
(called programmers) use a programming language to
communicate with a computer. You might have heard
of some of these languages in the past such as Visual
Basic, C++, or Fortran. There are hundreds of other
programming language and neither one is better than

the other. Most of them are capable of performing the same tasks and achieving the same goals. A programmer chooses one language by a simple preference.

Each of these languages differ by the way they communicate with a computer however, and the commands that they follow are very specific. Not a single command of one language can be interchanged with the commands or language of another. But all of them can be used to control a computer.

Now it would be impossible to teach you how to program any language in a single article. But we can still introduce you to some of programming's most basic concepts – starting with the commands we talked about earlier. Commands are the instructions that a computer follows to perform an action. [3] To make them work inside of a program, programmers assign commands to objects like buttons for example.

The commands in a program are pretty useless unless they have some data to act on so programmers either give the programs some data to work with (list of names or numbers for example) or they make the

---

program generate it's own data. Sometimes, the data comes from an outside source like the Internet or the computer that the program runs on. The data that a program receives is called input and data that the program generates is called output.

Other times, the data is unknown. If the program were working with a simple algebra equation like, "x + 5 = y," the variables "x" and "y" would be unknown pieces of data. Or if a program were to calculate a date "x" days from now, the variable "x" would be an unknown piece of data until we tell the program what "x" is. In programming, it's sometimes required to work with unknown pieces of data.

That's when conditions come in handy. Conditions allow a program to perform an action based on the outcome of a previous command.[4] Using this type of instruction, we could instruct a program to do one thing if the "x" variable in our latter example turned out to be 7 days, and then do different thing if the variable turned out to be 3 days.

Commands, data, variables, and conditions help build the most simple programs and there are certainly many more components of any programming language. But when they're typed into a programming language and compiled to create a an executable file (a file ending with the .exe extension), they turn into a software application.

As we mentioned earlier, you can use a programming language to control your computer. By using simple commands, you can program your computer to perform mathematical tasks, fill out web forms, compose an email message and send it off, or any number of other things. If you're interested, you may find Visual Basic is one of the most easiest programming languages to learn. Visual Basic is an object-oriented programming language and it automatically codes much of a program the minute a programmer drags a button onto a screen.

Networking Home Computers
Increasing Productivity With the Whole Family

Have you ever thought about networking your computers at home? If you have a small collection of computers around the house (and a small collection of computer users), you can connect each one of those computers to one another and share data, software, and hardware including a single Internet connection. There are many creative uses for home networking, however it's an ideal situation when upgrading each computer to the same capability is financially out of the question. On a home network, each computer has access to the equipment of the better machine in the group as if that equipment were their own.

Connecting computers with either an Ethernet cable or a Wireless connection can create a home network. The easiest and cheapest method uses an Ethernet connection, which requires a series of network cards, a cable for each computer, and a router. The network card is similar to the old modems we used in the past to connect to the Internet, however in a home network, it's used to communicate with every computer that's connected to it.

You'll want to first, select the computers that will connect to each other and then install the network cards inside each of them. Then you'll connect a cable to each computer that will communicate with the server. These cables won't connect to the server directly. Instead, they'll connect to the router. To enable Internet access for each computer, this router will need to connect with a modem of the host machine.

Once the hardware is set up correctly (you'll need to read the instruction manual of your equipment for details), you can then setup the network from Windows on each machine. Within Windows, you can set up a home network similar to the way that you set up an Internet connection. Only this time, you'll set up a LAN (Local Area Network) connection.

Windows should walk you through setting up a LAN after starting the computer and once complete, you can begin to connect one of your machines to the network. You can do this through Internet Explorer by typing in the address and password required to access the router (the address and password required to access the router will be in the router manual).

Connected to the network, each computer can send files back and forth, open programs on a remote computer, play the sound files and videos located on another computer, and share a single Internet account to browse the web, download files, or chat with someone in an entirely different country. If a single printer is available on only one computer in the network, every connected PC can send documents to it and print them out. Kids will enjoy the ability to play multi-player games and adults will enjoy the ability to blast a single message to everyone at once or maintain a group schedule.

Since we're describing a home network that will connect to the Internet, you're strongly advised to install a protective firewall program to thwart Internet viruses, worms, or other damaging spyware code. Firewalls prevent – but they don't repair. Only anti-virus and anti-spyware programs can reverse damage. So you should install a firewall on the computer that grants access to the computer, and then install an anti-virus and anti-spyware program on each of the remaining computers in the network.

If you have files that shouldn't be shared (bank statements, credit card information, etc.), you can restrict their access in one of several ways. You can put them in a new folder and then remove the "read" permissions for that folder. Or you can specify who can (and who cannot) access specific files with a password from within Windows Control Panel.

Open Source Software

If you've spent any lengthy amount of time on the Internet, you've probably heard of open source software but might not have fully understood what it is and why it even exists. This article will describe this recent phenomenon and describe some of its benefits for the software using community.

In a nutshell, open source software is software made by everyone – for everyone. The hopes behind its development is that through its open access, it will evolve into something that represents the true desires of computer users. Through a wide network of user involvement, the software in question is enhanced and debugged without costs or administrative politics.

Traditionally, software is developed behind closed doors. A team of professional coders build it but the community at large isn't part of its conception. It's costly to produce and as you can probably guess, that cost is passed on to the end user: the consumer. Open source software on the other hand is free. Free to download, free to install, free to use, free to modify, and free to share.

Started over twenty years ago, it's a phenomenon that is gaining in both popularity and exposure. In its first conception, open source gave birth to the World Wide Web as we know it today. The Internet as a whole is the result of free permission to access the web, use the web, contribute to the web, and share the web with others. But it certainly hasn't stopped there. In the not too distant past, Netscape converted its once commercial version of its Navigator web browser to open source. And today, open source is venturing into the commercial realm as well.

At first thought, the idea of open source may sound just plain crazy to those who earn a living from software development. But the facts point to a different prediction. Open source software puts companies in a terrific position to re-brand and re-position themselves in a market that they may have not been able to reach before. In the business world, open source is all about image and when consumers witness corporations contributing (instead of selling) to the buying public, they gain big favor in the eyes of their users (plus tremendous opportunities to sell other items).

Inviting the public inside a product's development builds community and trust. It also sets the platform for increased reliability. Fans of open source programs are adamant about reliable software and highly criticize commercialized versions for being buggy and error-prone. Avid fans even proclaim commercialism is the cause of shoddy software.

Another benefit that open source brings to light is the speed at which its products are developed, enhanced, supported and distributed. This is because the people who regularly contribute to an open source product do so for unmotivated reasons (other than perhaps to feed the ego.) They're highly talented, they're available, and they care. Bringing money into any project can almost mean instant death. It can kill motivation, desire, and a true willingness to create a good product. In a commercial setting, participants work for a paycheck rather than for the product. And this is what puts open source projects far ahead of its monetized competition.

As a software user, this means you can contribute to an open source project as well, and help to develop it into a product that reflects your direct preferences.

You aren't "stuck" using open source software the way you would be stuck using an expensive word processor or database. You have the same access to open source software as its programmers have and in essence, you are your own customer!

Perhaps at this point you're wondering where you can get in on this wonderful opportunity. There are plenty of open source opportunities sprinkled across the Internet and they can be easily found though any search engine. Google "open source project" and you'll be sure to find more resources than you can shake a stick at!

Protecting Children Online
Steps Toward Making Your Computer "Weirdo-Proof"

It's an unfortunate fact of reality, but children are the most victimized computer users on the Internet today. The good news is that there are some practical steps you can take to protect your children from sexual predators, hackers, and other seedy individuals who want to cause harm. This article will describe a few of them.

The first step in protecting your children at the computer is to prevent their access to passwords. This will keep them from sharing passwords with others and inadvertently enabling hacking into your system. If you think about it, there's no reason why a five, seven, or even twelve year old needs to know the passwords to sensitive areas on the computer unless you've given them permission! In fact, children don't need to know the password used to access the Internet either. It may be a hassle to type it in each time they want to get online, but it's better to know the times that they connect than to have them sneak online without your permission and knowledge of their activities.

The second step towards protecting your children online is using the computer together. Siting next to your child while he or she peruses the Internet, you can guide him or her to make safe and intelligent decisions. You can approve websites and bookmark them together. You can monitor the conversations your children have with their friends and teach them appropriate online behavior at the same time. You can make recommendations and create a private time for quality time as well.

The third step involves blocking access to inappropriate areas altogether. You and your children may not always agree about what's appropriate, but as a guardian, you're in control and you're ultimately responsible for their safety. Take the time to investigate software tools that put you in control and allow you to block access to certain websites. If you use an online service like AOL (America Online), you can use its internal Parental Control settings to block access to various chatrooms and websites. You could even block instant messaging and email from anyone who isn't a fellow AOL user.

Other tools available online operate similar to the way that AOL's Parental Control settings work, however no collection of tools could replace the reinforcement of mom and dad. Never let your children speak with strangers and never leave them alone at the computer unattended. Children just don't have the experience that adults have and they don't have the skills required to handle inappropriate conversations, emails, or images found online.

NOTE: Some of these tools include kid-specific web browsers that will visit pre-approved websites. Others include browser plug-ins that won't allow access to online areas that contain forbidden keywords.

Another step requires teaching your children to never ever volunteer personal information. Under no circumstances, should children give their personal names, home addresses, phone numbers, or school information to anyone over the Internet regardless of the situation. In the even this information is required to enter a contest of some sort, be sure that you're the one who makes the decision to supply it and that you're the one who does it.

Performing all of these steps won't be easy. However you can help minimize resistance to your monitoring efforts by explaining why you're taking these precautions. Smaller children will probably enjoy the time you spend together at the computer, but older children and pre-teens may resent it. To help build a case for your concern, you might want to show your older children a few news stories that exemplify the dangers that unsupervised children are exposed to. The newspaper is unfortunately full of examples but with your help, we can reduce them world-wide.

Selling Your Computer
Looking At Alternatives

At some point, your needs are going to outgrow the capabilities of your computer. You may find yourself in need of more hard drive space for all those videos and mp3s that you download, for example. Or maybe that cool new programming language you've been dying to try requires more memory than what your computer currently has. Unless the activities on your computer are restricted to pure textual output (plain text files), your computer is going to get filled with a lot of "stuff" – stuff that can overfill a PC's capacity too much for the computer to function well.

The problem is that while upgrading a computer is always an option, technology advances so fast that newer products (such as memory chips, new drives, etc.) aren't always compatible with the machines that we own. This is a common occurrence when newer pieces of hardware require the programming of a newer operating system. Sure, one could upgrade the operating system to accommodate the demands of a new piece of hardware, but trouble starts when that new operating system requires new hardware in return. If we're not careful, we could end up replacing almost every hard and soft part of a computer that we own – all in an effort to upgrade! Upgrading in this fashion is not only silly to do so, it's also costly – more costly than simply buying a new computer.

But once the decision to buy a computer is set in stone, what can be done with the old one? There are alternatives to selling a computer and this article is going to introduce a few of them.

1. Give it to the kids. This is of course, assuming the kids are too young to whine about not having enough SDRAM or less than a 160GB hard drive. Today's "older" computers are perfectly capable of accommodating the needs of young PC users, and they're excellent machines for playing educational CDs, small multimedia files, or games downloaded from the Internet. And don't forget the most important role they play in a child's homework-clad life: A simple encyclopedia CD on a used computer makes excellent research tool (not to mention a rather fancy calculator!).

2. Donate it to a less-fortunate or less-literate family member. We often joke around the office about the "grandma" who refuses to use a computer until she can afford the "latest" one. Chances are,

Grandma isn't ever going to shell out the bucks to buy the latest computer on the market, nor is she going to know how to use it once she gets it. What Grandma doesn't realize however is that a used computer is an excellent training tool that she can use to prepare herself for something "better" in the future. We always say, "'Tis better to screw up something on an old, used machine than to screw up everything on a brand new one!" A couple of errors on an old, used machine are easier to fix because someone is going to have the experience and knowledge to fix it. Errors on a new machine however can be a beast to fix because we're all knocking at Microsoft's door looking for answers.

3. Convert the machine into a storage area. As another alternative to selling that machine, we suggest that people disconnect it from the Internet and use it to store personal documents, records, or files. This way, personal data (such as bank statements, store receipts, health records, etc.) is protected from prying viruses or hackers, while the newer machine is used to surf the net.

As you can see, old computers still serve a purpose either for you or for someone else. And although selling an old computer is always an option, there are a number of things that you can do with an old computer. All that's required is a little "out of the box" thinking and a grateful recipient.

Smartphones

What's the craze all about?

If you haven't heard of smartphones, we'd like to learn where you've been hiding all this time. Smartphones have been all over the news and chances are, you do know what they are – only you know them under a different name. Smartphones are mobile phones with computer like capabilities.

What's that? Aha! Yes, you've not only heard of them, you've probably seen them as well. Packed with Internet access, email capabilities, address books, and a whole lot more, cell phones have come a long way since their first debut. But be careful not to confuse these newest toys with sandbox devices.

Sandbox devices are tools that come pre-loaded with things like calendars, calculators, and a notepad. What differentiates them from smartphones is that users can add (download and install) additional programs to smartphones and they seemingly become mini portable computers for the people who use them. That – and the ability to edit the content that sits on them - is what makes these phones "smart."

Some of the more popular brand names include the Blackberry, PalmSource, Nokia, and Windows CE. Yet the craze is extending to even some off-brand company names. Today, it's hard to find a cell phone that doesn't offer some sort of "smart" technology because it's in such a high demand. The convenience of having information at our immediate access is phenomenal – so much so that thousands of programmers have jumped on the opportunity to build unique applications specific to these small machines.

As a result, you can find tons of games, databases, GPA systems, weather reporting programs, and even small encyclopedias on these things – each accessible not at the click of a mouse – but at a few presses of a free thumb. Of course a mini keyboard is available for the text-messaging fan or for the poor fellow who can't seem to get away from the office. In the latter case, don't be surprised if you find the entire Microsoft Office suite displayed within a screen no bigger than a matchbook.

Is this a phase? That's highly doubtful. The market for these devices extends from the highly technical and professional all the way to the pre-teen socialite. The product crosses all demographics and thanks to decreasing costs – it sees no economic boundaries as well. The Wikipedia encyclopedia claims that "Out of 1 billion camera phones to be shipped in 2008, Smartphones, the higher end of the market with full email support, will represent about 10% of the market or about 100 million units."

But what is it that makes smartphones so appealing? As mentioned, smartphones give us the ability to not only carry our data around with us where ever we go, it also gives us the ability to edit that data any place – any time. In today's "reality" based generation, we're always looking for the opportunity to capture and relive a moment. And we want to share that moment with others. At best, smart phones give us the opportunity to express ourselves impromptu with entertaining results.

Attempting to do the same with a bulky desktop computer or laptop is to cumbersome. Even some of the smallest peripherals (digicams, digital cameras, etc.) don't give us the same opportunities that smart phones do. Being able to carry around a device for communication, creation, recording, and editing simply compliments the need for today's generation to do more and then do it, faster!

Software Piracy
It's Best To Avoid It At All Costs

Like electronic identity theft, computer viruses, and the spread of other computer crimes, software piracy is on the rise. The problem with software piracy is that software costs make this illegal activity appealing to the end user. After all, who is it going to hurt? Rich software companies?? This article investigates software piracy as a whole and the impact that it has on the computer using industry.

The most vulnerable victims of software piracy are software businesses or independent programmers who create and distribute commercial software or shareware. We described shareware in another article, but because both commercial software and shareware require payment, they're the target of pirates who seek to make these kinds of programs free to use.

Depending on their binding legal agreements, licensing typically allows the use of a single program on a single computer. This set up is usually fine for a user who uses software at home on one computer. But in an environment where there are five, ten, twenty or more computers, buying a license for each computer can be down-right costly. So costly that the temptation to pirate a little software here and there can be pretty tempting.

Co-workers are familiar with this temptation and they're often the ones who "share" purchased software among those who need it. However the same temptation also prompts others to knowingly or unknowingly buy bootleg copies of commercial software or registered shareware.

As tempting as it is, it's still illegal and the punishments/fines for sharing commercial or registered software is too much for one to bear. In recent news, "Yahoo China loses music piracy case (AP via Yahoo! News) A court has ordered Yahoo Inc.'s China subsidiary to pay $27,000 for aiding music piracy, the company and a music industry group said Tuesday."[5] Additionally, "EU lawmakers approve prison terms, fines for major commercial piracy (International Herald Tribune) EU lawmakers voted Wednesday for legislation that would set prison sentences and fines for large-scale commercial

_____

piracy, but exempt patents and copying carried out for personal use." [6]

Fortunately, there are alternatives. Schools can research student versions of commercial software or ask for a school discount. Just because school rates aren't advertised, it doesn't mean that they aren't available. Freeware or open source software (also described in another one of our articles) is another alternative to pirating commercial-ware, as well as shareware. And using older versions of programs could additionally reduce the costs associated with commercial versions.

Up until recently, public opinion held little faith in freeware or open source software – often regarding it as low-quality knock-off's of better known commercial products. But if you take a good look at what's being offered at no cost, you may be in for a big surprise. The quality of today's freeware and open source software created a strong rift among the commercial community and it's literally driving the competition bananas! So much so, that even some well known software development corporations have joined the cause and built a few freeware open source products of their own!

If you can remember that there are hoards of alternatives to costly commercial software (and you make the effort to get it), you'll discover that you can keep up with the rest of the computer industry at a significantly cheaper cost than if you attempted to pay your way down the software aisle. Software piracy just isn't the answer.

Understanding Compression
What It Is and What's Involved

Downloading files from the Internet has always been one of the most popular activities on the Internet – third to sending email and browsing the web. We download files from software libraries, ftp directories, YouTube and Google Video, MP3 sites, and we download files sent to us as email attachments.

Being so popular an activity, it's imperative that you compress the files destined for another computer. File compression combines a number of different files into one file, and it can also significantly reduce a very large file to a smaller one. As a result, the transmission of a compressed file across the Internet is faster and smoother. This article looks at compressed files a little closer and it describes how to compress and decompress them using two of the most popular archiving programs.

Identifying Compressed Files

Most files are compressed in .zip format (if you're using Windows) or .sit format (if you're using a Mac). The two most popular software programs used to compress and decompress files are Winzip and StuffIt respectively. There *are* other programs that do the same thing and there are even programs that can compress and decompress files for both the Windows and the Mac system. However since Winzip and StuffIt are the most popular, we will assume you will use either one to compress and decompress your own files.

If you download a compressed file from a website or file library that ends in an .exe extension, take note that although the file is compressed, it's typically a file that will install a program onto a computer. .Zip or .Sit files don't install software – they merely archive a collection of them into one, or they significantly reduce the size of a larger one.

Decompressing Files

Assuming that you have Winzip or StuffIt installed on your computer, you can access the files archived inside a .zip or .sit file by simply double-clicking the archive (a file ending in a .zip or .sit extension).

Double-clicking one of these kinds of files will open up a window that displays the contents of the archive. In most cases, you can double click a file inside this window to use it, or you can select it and drag the file to a folder to view later.

Depending on how you elected to install Winzip or StuffIt, you may be able to right-click a .zip or .sit file and have the program extract its contents into a new folder for you.

Compressing Files

When you want to upload a file or email a collection of files to a friend, it's best to archive it as a .zip or .sit file first. This will decrease the time it takes for your computer to send it elsewhere, and it will also decrease the time it takes for someone else to download it.

To create your own .zip or .sit file, you can select a single file or a group of files from within Explorer, and right-click the selection. Again, depending on how you installed Winzip or StuffIt, you can click the

"Add to Zip" or "Add to Sit" option and have these programs automatically archive the file(s) into one.

Some files compress better than others and in some instances, you may not notice that much of a difference. The files that compress the best are images, documents, and multimedia files. Executable files (files that end in an .exe extension) don't compress that well, however when they're archived with a sizable number of other files, they compress rather well. Go figure!

Understanding Operating Systems

Every new computer that's brought home from the store has an operating system installed onto it. But what most new computer users don't realize, is that without an operating system, that computer would be a simple shell of possibilities. A powered computer lacking an operating system wouldn't display anything more than a bunch of confusing text messages that describe the computer's boot process. At the very end of this process, the computer looks for an operating system and if not found, it will prompt the user to tell it where it is.

Earlier computers didn't have an operating system and if you have experience with the computers of the early eighties, you'll remember that most to them didn't even have a hard drive! These old computers booted an MS-DOS type operating system from drivers stored onto a floppy disk, and in order to use a program, users would remove the boot floppy and then insert a new floppy that contained the program. The floppy not only stored the program (word processor, spreadsheet, etc.), it also stored the drivers that the program needed to communicate with the computer's hardware. As you can imagine, the cumbersome process of switching from floppy to floppy prompted the birth of the operating system.

An operating system is a software program that controls how the computer's hardware (and installed software) works. It manages the activity of every component and then displays that activity as a user-friendly interface (GUI). It keeps track of where things exist on a computer's hard drive as well. But perhaps most importantly for the end-user, the operating system is responsible for translating commands issued with a keyboard and mouse into binary code (010110101 stuff) that can communicate with a set of speakers, a printer, a scanner, and more.

With an operating system installed onto a computer's hard drive, users no longer need to boot a computer with a floppy disk, nor do they need to run programs from a floppy disk. All the drivers of a program are stored onto the computer and used whenever a program is started.

Apple's Macintosh computer was among the first of a couple systems to establish a user-to-hardware relationship through a user-friendly interface. Today, we have quite a few operating systems. Some of the more popular ones are Windows Vista, Mac OS X, ZETA, IBM, Unix, and Linux. But even still, operating systems have extended onto to non-computer devices such as game consoles, portable music players, and PDAs. Regardless of the device, the operating system installed onto it serves the same purpose across the board: to enable user-to-hardware communication.

When you think about upgrading your computer to a new operating system, be careful to make sure that you have the necessary hardware components. We tried to upgrade one of our Windows 98 machines to Windows XP, but we were cautioned that the former may not be hardware compatible with XP technology. Apparently, the Windows XP operating system requires components that weren't developed at the time Windows 98 was distributed and if we were to install Windows XP on this machine anyway, the new operating system would look for hardware that the computer didn't have. And that would be an instant recipe for failure.

Also be careful about installing operating systems that are incompatible with existing hardware. The hardware of Macintosh computers is extremely different from the hardware of Windows computers and under no circumstances will a Windows operating system work on a Macintosh machine!

Using Computers
It's Not Rocket Science

These days it's strange to hear people say, "I'm just not computer literate," as computers have evolved from archaic scientific calculators to simple point-and-click type machines. We suspect that today's "computer illiterates" are people who haven't taken the time to experiment with such a machine. And we strongly believe that spending just twenty minutes with one could turn the most adamant technological caveman into any one of those who have fun wreaking chatroom havoc on the Internet today.

Today, one only needs to learn how to manipulate a mouse, punch a few buttons on a keyboard, or really just turn the thing on to use a computer. It's hard for some folks to believe, but the computers of this generation almost run themselves! For fun, let's investigate just how little knowledge these thousand-dollar machines actually require.

Can an absolute newbie operate a computer without knowing how to use a mouse or keyboard? Assuming that a computer is set up to operate on voice command – sure! Voice command software allows users to tell a computer what to do and the computer responds by fulfilling the user's commands. Although it's pretty new and still under development, voice directed technology has already infiltrated consumer service related systems.

Think back to the last time that you paid a bill over the phone. Instead of speaking to a human being, chances are that you spoke to a computer that not only responded to what you said and followed the commands that you gave it, it also asked you for more information such as your full name or credit card number. In this case, a person (such as yourself) operated a computer without even knowing it!

Can an absolute newbie sit down at a computer without knowing how to use one? Assuming that a computer is set up to operate on touch command – the answer is again, yes! Touch command software allows users to literally touch objects on a monitor and tell the computer what to do with a finger. Known as "kiosks," these programs are already in use world wide at ATM machines, employment centers, and in health monitoring systems.

Neither a mouse nor a keyboard is required. A computer user only needs to touch various boxes on a screen to control a computer. Sure, the programming behind such technology is extensive and advanced, but to the end user, it makes computer use less intimidating and plain easy.

Of course when we talk about operating a computer, we envision more involvement than speaking on the phone or touching things on a screen. The above illustrations were just a couple of examples of how far computer technology has grown, and how far we've pushed "user-friendliness" to its limit. Eventually, the keyboard and mouse will have to play a role when computer newbies have to work with one as a cash register, as a hotel booking program, or as a library's catalog system.

These requirements don't make computers any less easier to operate, but they don't make them that much harder either. So much of today's software is designed to accommodate the experience of a new user that anyone could get connected to the Internet, send an email message, and download an MP3 file within the first five hours of purchasing a personal PC.

Viruses
What They Are And One Reason Why People Make
Them

Over recent years, computers have become
synonymous with viruses and viruses don't show any
signs of disappearing any time soon. In recent news,
LiveScience.com reported that "Before the month is
even done, April has set a record for virus e-mails."[7]
In the past, we would be comfortable in telling new
computer users not to worry about viruses and that
catching a computer virus is rare. Today, that would
be some of the worst advice we could give anyone. As
reported in countless news reports, computer viruses
are rampant and they're extremely worrisome. This
article will describe what viruses are and then point
you in the direction of some rather unique protection
and prevention.

In short, a computer virus is a software program
designed to destroy or steal data. It attacks computers
via distribution – often unknowingly – through email
attachments, software downloads, and even some
types of advanced web scripting. Viruses that destroy

data are known as Trojan horses, viruses that explode their attacks are called bombs, and viruses that duplicate themselves are called worms. Some viruses are a combination of each, however they can be further identified according to where they're located on a computer.

A virus originating from the boot sector of a computer is a boot-sector virus and this nasty devil does its dirty work the moment a computer is turned on. A virus that attaches itself to (infects) other programs is a file virus and activates the moment that an infected program starts. File viruses may also be referred to as parasitic viruses, however should a virus work from both the boot-sector and from an infected program, the virus is then known as a multipartite virus.

Why viruses exist remains a mystery, however we had privy access to the mind behind a virus programmer who explained his motivation behind his destructive inclinations. Apparently, this person had a deep grudge against a popular online service which shall remain unnamed. In this hacker's mind, the online service failed to do a quality job in protecting children from online smut and as retaliation, he created and distributed a virus to as many file libraries of this service as he could. His intentions were to disable the computers of the online service's users so much that they wouldn't be able to connect for days. In his mind, the loss of connection meant loss of revenue for the online service.

Although the malicious code that this person generated may have worked for a small percentage of users, sufficed to say, the online service continued on and still exists today. Despite his motivation or intention, his efforts were null.

We wouldn't be surprised to learn if other motivations behind spreading viruses were similar to this person's, but that doesn't justify the damage that viruses do. Innocent people become pawns for the evil plans of others who've convinced themselves they're doing the "right" thing.

To protect a computer from getting a virus, or clean a virus from a computer system once infected requires the use of an antivirus utility. But may be something else we can do. Perhaps we could make an effort to educate the people who want put viruses into the public about ways to display dissatisfaction with a service or product that don't involve harming innocent parties. In doing so, we just might reduce the number of virus news stories and protect our own investments at the same time.

What's That File?

An Introduction to File Extensions

In an effort to be "user-friendly," Windows (and perhaps some other operating systems) hides the most important part of a file name from new computer users: the extension. Okay – we're *assuming* that the reasoning behind hiding extensions is a "user-friendly" one because we just can't come up with any other reason for hiding them. No harm could ever come from seeing an extension, but plenty could be learned from it. Fortunately you have this article to guide you through some of the most common extensions that you'll run into.

But before you can see file extensions, you need to turn them on. From Windows Explorer, click on the "Tools" menu, and select "File Options." Click the "View" tab and then uncheck the box next to "Hide file extensions for known file types." Click "OK" and you'll notice that the files in Windows Explorer show a dot and group of three letters after their names. That dot and group of three letters is known as an "extension," and the extension explains what kind of file it is.

A file could be a plain text file, an image, a sound, a video, or program. But without seeing the extension, you wouldn't know it unless you double-clicked on it. The following list defines some of the most common extensions that you'll find on your computer.

.au – This extension indicates a sound file. Most sound players will load up and play this kind of file.

.art - This extension indicates an image file that was compressed with AOL (America Online) technology. Both Internet Explorer and the AOL service software can display this kind of file, however if you don't have AOL installed on your system, Internet Explorer will display it.

.avi - This extension indicates a video file playable by most multimedia viewers including Microsoft's Media Player.

.bmp - This extension indicates another image file that might have originated from Windows Paint program.

.dll - This extension indicates a Dynamic Link Library which may contain additional programming code for software. Many different programs often share Dynamic Link Libraries and you'll find a bunch of them in the Windows/System directory (but don't ever delete them)!

.exe - This extension indicates a program or an application like Microsoft Word, Internet Explorer, or Outlook Express. Use extreme caution when downloading .exe files from the Internet since malicious programmers like to hide viruses in these types of files.

.gif - This extension indicates another image file and it stands for "Graphics Interchange Format." .Gif files are often smaller than .bmp files (described earlier) and they're commonly found on Internet web pages.

.jpg - This extension indicates yet another image file and it stands for "Joint Photographers Experts Group." Like the .gif file, it's commonly found on Internet web pages, however it's much smaller than both the .gif image and the .bmp image.

.mid - This extension indicates a sound file created with a Musical Instrument Digital Interface. Windows Media Player will open and run these files, however they don't sound like normal .wav or .mp3 files (described later). .Mid files are designed to product synthetic sounds using a computer's sound card.

.mp3 - This extension indicates a sound file that authentically reproduces voice and/or music. Windows Media Player will open and run this kind of file.

.scr - This extension indicates a screen saver file.

.sit - This extension indicates a Macintosh archive StuffIt file. They will not open on a Windows system without a special utility.

.ttf - This extension indicates a font especially designed for use on a Windows system. It stands for "True Type Font."

.txt - This extension indicates a plain text file that can be opened with Notepad.

.wav - This extension indicates a sound file that like the .mp3 file, can be opened with Windows Media Player or Windows Sound Recorder. .Wav files are much larger than .mp3 files.

.zip - This extension indicates a Windows archive WinZip file. They will not open on a Macintosh system without a special utility.

When Less Is More
Clean Your Disk Drive of Unnecessary Files and Your
Computer's Performance Will Improve

When it comes to maintaining your computer, you've probably heard it all before. "Run Defrag!" "Scan Your Disk for Errors!" Although these two activities are important, there's more you can do to extend the life of your computer beyond today's predicted two-year span. In fact, by following the simple advice below, you can enjoy the use of your computer to up to five years or more – reserving expenses to simple software upgrades rather then complete and costly hardware upgrades.

One of the easiest and least expensive things you can do to extend the life of your computer is to get rid of unnecessary programs, folders, and files. A disk drive that's clogged with unnecessary and unused files is disk drive that works harder than it has to. Although Window's defrag system can ease some of the stress that these files place onto the drive, it doesn't do much to get rid of the problem in the first place. This is because the defrag program simply organizes the files in a system that makes it easier for the computer to access. (Thus cutting down on the work required to find and load them). But this method merely "relieves" the symptoms that these files induce – it doesn't attack the cause. These files need to be deleted – not "organized!"

Of course, deleting files can be a scary adventure to most users. Most computer users don't know which files are safe to delete and which aren't.

The worst thing anyone could do is snoop around crucial Window directories and haphazardly delete files that don't look familiar. Doing so could render important programs inoperable, corrupt the Windows operating system, and possibly prevent the computer from even starting. That's why using special deletion software is so important. Deletion programs will analyze a computer's operating system and installed programs to determine which files are crucial to computer function versus which files are safe to delete.

You already have such a program on your computer and it's Windows' Add/Remove Programs (available from the Control Panel). This software will assist you with deleting programs that you not only no longer want, but additional files that these program use as well (dynamic link libraries, database files, registry references, shortcut icons, etc.).

But sometimes Windows' Add/Remove Programs isn't enough. Although this software does a pretty good job of removing unwanted programs, it can leave some files behind even after a complete uninstall – files which become orphan files. And it's these orphan files that can really clutter up a hard drive and shorten the life of an otherwise, young and robust PC.

Orphans are usually files that contain temporary data created by a program, files created by the user, partial files left over from a computer crash, or any other kind of miscellaneous files created for almost any other reason. The problem is that an uninstall program doesn't delete the orphan files it leaves behind because they were never part of the program when it was first installed. An uninstall program can remove only the files it placed onto a hard drive during its install routine.

So while Windows' Add/Remove Programs can remove an entire program, you'll need to get rid of those pesky little things with a more advance file cleaner like CleanSweep for example. CleanSweep is a unique program that will specifically seek out files that are no longer associated with a program, and then ask if you want to delete them.

The only time that you wouldn't want to delete an orphan file is if the file were an actual document that you created before deleting a program. If you were to say, uninstall Microsoft Word, all the documents that you created with Word would then turn into orphan files. Or if you were to uninstall a graphics-editing program, all the pictures you made with the program would become orphan files.

The smart thing to do when you don't want to lose the data that you created with an unwanted program is to:

1. Save or convert your documents to a format that will work with different program first (that is, a program that you intend to keep)
2. Archive them onto a floppy disk, flash drive, or CD-ROM
3. Proceed with a program like CleanSweep.

Using CleanSweep or any other similar type of utility could delete anywhere from less than a megabyte of hard drive space to over five megabytes and up. That may seem like a small amount of "clog material" to you, but to your computer, it's a lot less to process!

Working With Computers
In Today's Society, There's No Escape

Well, we've been warned that this time would come –
probably from the earlier eighties on. Yes, computers
have finally taken over and if you doubt it, we're here
to convince you - but not because we want to or
because we can. We want to convince you that if you
don't take the necessary steps to control that reign,
you're going to be left behind further than you could
have ever imagined.

Computers are everywhere. Take a moment to try
and think of a place a business where you didn't see a
computer in use. From the small local corner store to
the largest hospital, computers are in every gas
station, grocery store, bank, restaurant, beauty shop,
and doctor's office around. From a consumer's point
of view – you may not think that's much to worry
about. But along with computers, we've also been
infiltrated with a little thing called "self-service."
Today, there are more self-serviced resources than
ever and in an effort to synchronize them with
headquarter databases, they're provided via your
inescapable computer.

Here are some examples. Banking is self-serviced through the desktop-clad ATM machine. Gas stations are self-serviced through a menu-clad touch screen kiosk. Most cash registers are Windows XP or Vista machines that send purchase details back to headquarters via the Internet (or a small Intranet). Having your weight, blood pressure, and heart rate measured and recorded is now a digitized process. Even ordering a pizza is now a simple matter of dialing from a wireless cell phone and making a few selections from series of pre-programmed menus!

The important thing to realize here is that this phenomenon isn't a new convenience – it's a new requirement. And if you haven't jumped onto the binary wagon, you're going to face a few problems. For just as this new lifestyle was once predicted, we're going to predict that "the old ways" will slowly disappear.

We're going to predict that all paper-based transactions (checks, money orders, etc.) and documentation (think of the old filing cabinet system) will disappear. We're going to predict that chips will replace everything that was once transported from one location to another through the trusty post office. And we're going to predict that homes will become less cluttered with stacks of paper and that our natural resources will flourish as a result of it.

This all sounds fine and dandy of course, but if you're not computer savvy, you're going to feel a little lost once the choice has past and the revolution is 100% complete. Fortunately, computer systems are designed in a way that even a child can manipulate them. In fact, if you can remember that most systems are designed along the line of menus and the selections of a few options on these menus, you'll do just fine no matter how many buttons there are to push.

For example, when you're faced with an electronic system, look for a main menu. Most main menus display themselves as soon as a device is turned on, so chances are that if you're standing before a device that shows a bunch of choices to do something, you're looking at a main menu. The buttons on these main menus of course take you to additional menus, which in turn give you even more choices to make. And all of those choices will eventually bring you to the service that you need. One very important choice you'll want to keep your eye on is the option to return to the main menu. This way, you can return to the beginning of a system and start over in case you get lost among the way.

Another important choice that you want to keep your eye on is the choice to get help! This option may not be available on every device that you encounter, but when it is available, be sure to use it.

There's just no way around it. Computers and computerized systems are here to stay. There's no need to fear them – but you surely can't avoid them. Just remember the menu system and you'll soon discover that you can approach and use these things as if you designed them yourself.

www.ingramcontent.com/pod-product-compliance
Lightning Source LLC
Chambersburg PA
CBHW031244050326
40690CB00007B/948